AF409991

THE NOT SO GREAT DIVIDE

Exploring the Femininity to Masculinity Spectrum of Personality

Jon Coley

THE NOT SO GREAT DIVIDE

First edition. June 5, 2023.

Copyright © 2023 Jon Coley.

ISBN: 979-8223091820

Written by Jon Coley.

In memory of my cousin, Beth. I think you were right. I think it's stumble.

Part One Conception

Sheldon: Are you speaking figuratively or would you like to do the math?

Leonard's mom: I'd like to do the math.

Chapter 1 - Why?

The lines above from the sitcom, The Big Bang Theory, are illustrious of the super nerdy experience I had when deciding to write this book. You see, I was planning on writing a nice little kids fiction middle grades novel about a suicidal squirrel (yes, really). I had already written a book about personality typing and how it could be applied in the kindergarten through twelfth grade classroom. Thinking everything that needed to be said had been ... said, I was content to shift back into fiction writing mode again. Then I saw it. A YouTube channel that I enjoy following called AsuraPsych discussed the masculinity and femininity tendencies of certain types. Well, I had already heard others in the MBTI community, like ObjectivePersonality.com[1], discussing this issue, but this was different. Sure, both parties had some points that seemed dubious, but both also made compelling arguments too. At any rate, it got me to thinking, which is always dangerous.

Wanting to get the thought out of my head, I decided to write a short blogpost about it on my author website, www.joncoleyauthor.com[2]. That was a big mistake. Like Leonard's mother, I wanted to do the math. Said math was done forthwith, and the results both fascinated and surprised me. In some ways, for such is the condition of exploration in the softer sciences, there were more questions than answers. Another way to put this is that I could be totally wrong. So why write a book about it? In short, I think I'm on to something and it would be great if others with more scientific minds looked at it. There are a ton of caveats that go with this writing. They

---

1.   http://ObjectivePersonality.com

2.   http://www.joncoleyauthor.com

are painfully obvious, and I won't waste anyone's time writing about them in this chapter. For now, let it be said that this book merely poses a question and conducts a thought experiment with the Myers-Briggs Type Indicator in light of masculinity and femininity. In short, I did the math so you don't have to.

Some readers put this book down when they saw the word, math. Can't say I blame them. Some of them saw MBTI, rolled your eyes, and walked away. What can I say? It's not for everyone. As for the rest of you, thank you for taking a look. Let me assure you that I know that math makes a boring read and that MBTI isn't considered scientific by some (or many). Well, there isn't that much math in this book, anyway. Plus it's not by any measure high level thinking. Not to mention, you don't have to do it. I did. Also, MBTI is the most popular and accessible personality typing system out there. It has a thriving community for a reason. It is sound theory that is based on Jungian psychology. Like some of your parents may have said - try it. You might like it.

Jungian psychology changed my life. I related to it and was able to understand more about myself and others too. It's a profoundly illuminating way of looking at the world. Don't get me wrong, it's not a religion. It won't save your soul. Personality psychology, specially MBTI, is more than helpful, however, and provides insights into the human experience that would not otherwise be known. If you're new to personality typing, this book will be easy enough to follow because I'm a simple person. The different personality types will be discussed and explained fairly thoroughly. Plus this new question concerning masculinity and femininity will be addressed. I truly intend for every page to be pleasant to read and (hopefully) informative too. Here's the hook, you just might find out why you're different than everyone else. Also, you will get a feel for how others are thinking and where they're coming from.

The second chapter will be the math heaviest portion of the book. Their will be an introverted an explanation of the methodology. If it helps, just imagine a really nerdy professor with his shirt half untucked and a stain on his tie. Then the third chapter will lay out brief descriptions of the cognitive functions and assign the very simple mathematical formula I devised to address the question being explored in this book. And just like that, part one will be in the rear view mirror.

The chapters in parts two, three, and four will describe the personality types from masculine to balanced to feminine based on the continuum explained in part one. There will be very little math from here on out, but plenty of MBTI.

Finally, part five will contain a few chapters discussing what all this means, and will look to see if the book's assertions are even correct by taking a gander at personality types in the population. Don't hold me to this, but there will probably be some appendices at the end too with real charts and stuff.

So dear reader, that's what you're in for if you decide to read this book. I'm writing it because I have to. There's no way to describe how exhausting it is to have an entire nonfiction book stuck in your head. You don't have to read it, but I hope you do. It is my sincere belief that it is worth your time.

Chapter 2 - Methodology

This is the way.

- The Mandalorian

Before diving too deep, it's important to have better definitions for masculinity and femininity. These terms don't necessarily mean manliness or the opposite in the context of personality. These are more philosophical terms, such as described in Taoism. Full disclosure, I'm not a Taoist. I'm a Spirit filled Christian. But the Taoist philosophy puts forth the best way of understanding the concepts being discussed in this book. A flip in thinking may be needed here too. Many men would think they are masculine because they are men and women are feminine because they are women. But for the purposes in this discussion, it would be more accurate to say that most masculine people happen to be men and most feminine people happen to be women. The sexes generally fall in line between these two philosophical energies, but EVERYONE has some of both energies. Also, this book will not discuss sexual orientation in any form or fashion. Dave and Shannon at ObjectivePersonality.com[3] do discuss this subject a little on their YouTube channel if that's what floats your boat.

What is masculinity? Masculinity is a group of tendencies, behavior patterns, or energies. Some of these characteristics include logical thought, focus on goals, competition, support, assertiveness, outward focus of energy, and other traits.

What is femininity? Femininity is the opposite group of energies or behavior patterns. Traits like collaboration, nurturing, introspection, intuitive thought, passiveness, and many others make up this set of behavior patterns.

---

3.   http://ObjectivePersonality.com

Again, every one has some to all of these traits in their personality. The difference is that they will have a majority, or strength, in one energy and a minority, or weakness, in the other. Thus we have the image of the Yin and Yang fish swimming together in the circle of life.

Enter the MBTI community. Over time, it has been noticed by some of the more observant personality psychology geeks that the cognitive functions (more about this in the next chapter) are either more masculine or more feminine in nature. They inherently lean a certain way. For instance, most extroverted (outward functions) are masculine, while most introverted functions are feminine. Intuitive functions seem to be feminine, while sensing functions are generally more masculine. Thinking functions are masculine, and feeling (values) functions are feminine. Judging functions (not judgmental) are mostly masculine. Perceiving functions are feminine for the most part. Taking these characteristics into account, one can assign overall masculinity or femininity to each function. Moreover, their place in the cognitive stack (more on this later too) can be a multiplier of sorts for the dominance of each function in a given personality type. In other words, a person with a dominant function that is masculine will have more masculine tendencies in his or her personality, even though the other functions may be feminine, and vice versa.

Okay, stop. Let's get out of the weeds here. Long story short, I did the math. It looks like this:

$(4P)+(3S)+(2T)+(I)=R$

The P is the primary cognitive function, which is the most developed, so its value is multiplied by four, the lion's share. The S is the secondary function that develops in adolescence to early adulthood, so its value is multiplied by three. The T is the tertiary function, which is only developed in full adulthood, thereby only being multiplied by two. Finally the I is the inferior function, the least developed of the stack. It isn't multiplied at all. As anyone can see, this is a very simple formula for a very simple idea. It's not rocket science.

Every personality type has four active cognitive functions. The next chapter will explain what they are and give their ranking (which is what the R stands for in the formula). When assigning numbers to the functions, I discovered a continuum of negative three to positive three. Negative three being the most feminine and positive three being the most masculine.

By the way, this is not to say that feminine energy is negative. I was going left to right and I'm a gentleman, so ladies first.

-3 -2 -1 0 1 2 3

Most Feminine Neutral Most Masculine

How are these numbers assigned? If a function is extroverted, it gets a positive one, negative one if introverted. An intuitive function gets a negative one, while sensing functions get a positive one. Judging functions add one, while perceiving functions subtract one. Feeling functions are subtracted by one, thinking functions are added by one. Each function has three characteristics. If all three are feminine, like Introverted iNtuition, it gets a score of negative three. If two are negative, but one is positive, the score for that function is negative one, and so on.

Once these values are plugged into the formula, a composite ranking of negative six to positive six can be observed. Negative six is the personality type having the most feminine qualities. Positive six is the ranking of the most masculine aligned personality type. These are not very big numbers, hence the title of the book.

That's it. That's the methodology. If you're new to the MBTI system, you have no idea what I'm talking about. Don't worry. After explaining he cognitive functions, each personality type will be briefly described. There are only sixteen of them. Then the formula will be applied and their rankings on the Feminine to Masculine spectrum will be revealed. If what I've written sounds like gobbledygook so far, it will make more sense soon. I promise.

Chapter 3 - Cognitive Functions

Science is a way of thinking much more than it is a body of knowledge.

- Carl Sagan

The eight cognitive functions are listed below. A brief description is given for each, but there is far more to a cognitive function than what is provided in this book. This is, however, a good way to get the gist of each one. The ranking on the continuum is also given with a brief explanation.

Introverted iNtuition (Ni):

This cognitive function is a way of taking in information, also known as a perceiving function. It consists of advanced pattern recognition and gut reactions. It is able to make often unseen connections and to extrapolate their ramifications into the future.

Being a perceiving, intuitive, introverted function, it scores a rank of negative three. This is the most feminine cognitive function.

Extroverted iNtuition (Ne):

This function takes in information based on pattern recognition and connections, but is outwardly focused. Ne users often make seemingly random connections to a wide variety of things, situations, and abstract ideas.

It's an intuitive and perceiving function, but is extroverted - negative two plus one equals negative one. This unicorn is the only feminine extroverted function.

Introverted Sensing (Si):

This is an inward focused perceiving function that takes in sensory information and details in real time and subconsciously compares it all to past information, or the way things ought to be. It's concrete in nature and depends highly on memory.

Si is an introverted perceiving function, so negative two. But it's also a sensing function, so plus one. Negative two plus one is is negative one, which makes Si a feminine function.

Extroverted Sensing (Se):

This function takes in information from the outside world through the five senses and the other lesser known senses like proprioception, reaction to atmospheric pressure, and temperature. Everyone receives information through their senses, but Se users are very attentive to the present environment in great detail.

Se is a perceiving function, so negative one. It's extroverted and sensory, so positive two. Two subtract one is one. Thus, Se is the only masculine perceiving function. It's the other unicorn.

Introverted Thinking (Ti)

This function is inward focused and based on logic. It understands systems and the way things work. Rationale is more important than emotions or values when it comes to making decisions. Note, this logic can be objective or subjective in nature.

Ti is an introverted function, so negative one. It's also a thinking and judging function, so plus two. Two minus one is one, so Ti is the only introverted masculine function. Okay, so everybody's a unicorn.

Extroverted Thinking (Te)

Te is outward focused logic and organization. It creates systems to make things work more efficiently. It is rational and fair. Decisions are made using logic first and emotions last.

Te is an extroverted, thinking, and judging function, so plus three. Hence, Te is the most masculine function.

Introverted Feeling (Fi)

This function focuses inwardly on personal values and emotions. It's like a filter perceiving the world and deciding, "This is me," or "This isn't me." Decisions are made with intrinsic values and consideration of personal feelings before logic is considered.

Fi is introverted and feeling (duh), so negative two. It's also a judging function, so plus one. Negative two plus one equals negative one, so it's a feminine function.

Extroverted Feeling (Fe):

This function is focuses on the harmony and ambience of the group. Decisions are made based on the common values of the tribe.

Fe is an extroverted judging function, so plus two. It's also a feeling function, so minus one. Two minus one is positive one, so Fe is a masculine function.

That's it. That's all eight of them. Remember, there's a lot more to a cognitive function than the brief descriptions given above. Each one could, and perhaps does, have an entire book written about it. These brief descriptions are just a way to help you read the MBTI system's basic road map for the human brain.

We now have a continuum, and I get to make a chart! The cognitive functions and their feminine to masculine rankings are shown below.

Feminine		Neutral		Masculine	
-3	-2 -1	0	1 2 3		
Ni	Fi		Fe	Te	
	Si		Ti		
	Ne		Se		

There will likely be another chart listing each personality type with its ranking on the femininity to masculinity spectrum at the end of this book. If that's your kind of thing, you're going to love it. This is the end of Part One. Part Two will cover those testosterone loving masculine personality types.

Part Two
Masculine Types

Chapter 4 - ISTP and ISTJ

He who works with his hands and his head and his heart is an artist.

- Saint Francis of Assisi

Sports teaches you character. It teaches you to play by the rules. It teaches you what it feels like to play by the rules. It teaches you about life.

- Billie Jean King

The first two masculine personality types are THE CRAFTER and THE INSPECTOR. These are the only two introverts on the masculine side of the continuum. On a scale from negative six to positive six, they rank at positive two, meaning they certainly possess both kinds of energies, but are placed squarely masculine category.

ISTP - THE CRAFTER

Introverted-Sensor-Thinker-Perceiver

The primary function of this type is introverted thinking, or Ti. The secondary function is extroverted sensing (Se). The tertiary function is introverted intuition (Ni), and rounding the personality type out is extroverted feeling, or Fe.

These people usually don't mind working alone and with their hands, like a mechanic or woodworker. They also like to live in-the-moment. Usually being a good type to have around during an emergency, first responders and emergency room doctors have been recommended careers for them. They also prefer a flexible approach to life. A good example of this type would be Schroeder from Charles Schultz' Peanuts franchise.

Here's the math:

(1x4)+(1x3)-(3x2)+(1)

4+3-6+1

7-6+1

1+1

2 - masculine

ISTJ - THE INSPECTOR

Introverted-Sensor-Thinker-Judger

With only one different letter, you have a completely different personality type. The ISTJ leads with introverted sensing (Si). The secondary function is Te, or extroverted thinking. Introverted feeling (Fi) is the tertiary function in the stack, and the inferior function is Ne, or extroverted intuition.

These are hard working, stick to rules, nose to the grindstone people. They are the foot soldiers of daily battle. A surprising ISTJ fictional character (because he doesn't look the stereotypical part) would be Severus Snape from JK Rowling's Harry Potter franchise. Believe me, that last statement will give conniptions to some muggles in the MBTI community. But it's true - ALWAYS.

Vague fanboy jokes aside, here's the math:

(-1x4)+(3x3)-(2x1)-(1x1)

-4+9-2-1

5-3

2 - masculine

Once again, these were the only two introverted types on the masculine side of the spectrum. All the rest are extroverts, as one may expect. The only surprise I found was that one personality type is a feeler, but that will be covered in the next chapter.

Chapter 5 - ENTJ and ESFP

There is no security on this earth; there is only opportunity.

- General Douglas MacArthur

The whole world is a stage, and all the men and women are merely actors.

- William Shakespeare

It is not surprising that THE FIELD MARSHAL (aka THE EXECUTIVE) is a masculine type, but THE ENTERTAINER is a feeler and perceiver. Be that as it may, both these types have a positive four ranking on the spectrum.

ENTJ - THE EXECUTIVE
Extroverted-iNtuitive-Thinker-Judger

Just as the nickname implies, people with this type are born leaders. Their primary function is extroverted thinking (Te), which lends to excellent decision making skills, especially for the outside tribe. The secondary function, introverted iNtuition (Ni), helps them to form deep insights in any situation or organization. The tertiary slot is Se, or extroverted sensing, helping them to pay attention to their surroundings and to their colleagues. Lastly, they have introverted feeling (Fi), which allows them, with effort, to develop strong core beliefs.

My father-in-law, who is one of my favorite people, is an ENTJ. He was indeed an executive in the finance industry for decades. A more famous example would be Alexander Hamilton. Many in the MBTI community believe this Founding Father was this personality type based on his history and writings. I wonder what Aaron Burr's type was.

Here's the math:

(4x3)-(3x3)+(2x1)-(1x1)

12-9+2-1

3+1

4 - masculine

ESFP - THE ENTERTAINER

Extroverted-Sensor-Feeler-Perceiver

The Entertainer's lead function is extroverted sensing (Se). This means they are active in the world and are living very much in-the-moment. Fi, or introverted feeling is their secondary function, giving them ample capacity to develop strong core values and to make decisions based on them. Their tertiary function is extroverted thinking (Te), which helps them to organize their outside world and make logical decisions, though only after their Fi has a say in the matter. The inferior function is Ni, or introverted intuition. Being the least developed of the four in the stack, this function helps them to trust their gut, but is developed over a lifetime of experience.

Charlie Brown's friend, Freida with the naturally curly hair, is a good example of an ESFP. Many people also consider Will Smith and Marilyn Monroe to be ESFP's.

Here's the math:

$(4x1)-(3x1)+(3x2)-(3x1)$

$4-3+6-3$

$1+3$

4 - masculine

Chapter 6 - ESTP and ESTJ

What separates the winners from the losers is how a person reacts to each new twist of fate.

- President Donald Trump

If they ask you to convert Fahrenheit to Celsius, remember that it's easier just to put on a sweater.

- Peppermint Patty

The two types ranking the highest on the masculinity side of the scale are nicknamed THE NEGOTIATOR and THE MANAGER. While most of their preferences are the same, one is a perceiver and the other a judger, which changes their cognitive functions. Be that as it may, they both ranked at positive six on the masculinity side of the spectrum, the highest score possible.

ESTP - THE NEGOTIATOR

Extroverted-Sensor-Thinker-Perceiver

The Negotiator's primary function is extroverted sensing (Se), which places them very much in the present, taking in the world around them and continually processing that information in great detail. The secondary function is Ti, or introverted thinking, which is internally focused logic and problem solving. Extroverted feeling (Fe) is the tertiary function, gauging the ambience and morale of the tribe. The inferior function is introverted intuition (Ni), helping the negotiator to learn to trust his/her gut and to pick up on the occasional pattern or new opportunity.

The most famous negotiator right now would be President Donald Trump, believed to be an ESTP. One would only have to read "The Art of the Deal" to see that this is his personality type. Other less political ESTP examples would include Angelina Jolie and Jack Nicholson.

Here's comes that math:

(1x4)+(1x3)+(1x2)-(3x1)

4+3+2-3

4+2

6 - masculine

ESTJ - THE MANAGER

Extroverted-Sensor-Thinker-Judger

The Manager's primary function is Te, or extroverted thinking. This is the most masculine of all the functions, organizing and systematizing the outside world. The secondary function is introverted sensing (Si), a feminine function that depends greatly on memory, and is continually comparing information from the outside world to the way things were in the past or the way things ought to be. The tertiary function is extroverted intuition (Ne), the only feminine extroverted function, recognizing connections between seemingly unrelated things in the outside world. Finally, the inferior function is Fi, or introverted feeling, which is related to inner values.

Peppermint Patty from the Peanuts franchise is a good example of this personality type. Rewatch "A Charlie Brown Thanksgiving " to see these cognitive functions on full display.

Here's the math:

(3x4)-(3x1)-(2x1)-(1x1)

12-3-2-1

9-3

6 - masculine

Part Three
Balanced Types

24

Chapter 7 - ISFJ and INTP

If you can't explain it simply, you don't understand it well enough.

- Albert Einstein

Life sucks, but in a beautiful kind of way.

- Axl Rose

This chapter consists of the two introverted types whose masculine and feminine energies are balanced. This is the term I decided to use instead of a term like neutral, because I do not believe the energies and behaviors cancel one another out. They are all present in a given personality type. Part Two of this book consisted of personality types that simply had more masculine energy than feminine, but the feminine energy is still there and observable. After doing the math, four types were found with balanced energy, two introverted and two extroverted. Without further delay, I present a THE DEFENDER and THE ARCHITECT.

ISFJ - THE DEFENDER

Introverted-Sensor-Feeler-Judger

The Defender's primary function is introverted sensing (Si), which is memory driven and always comparing the outside world to how things were in the past, or the way things ought to be. That's what they feel responsible for defending. Extroverted feeling (Fe) is the secondary function that focuses on the values and the morale of the tribe. Ti, or introverted thinking, is the tertiary function, using logic to analyze circumstances, systems, and situations. The inferior function is Ne, or extroverted intuition, recognizing connections, possibilities, and patterns between seemingly random abstract things and ideas.

The ISFJ is a defender of the way things ought to be. They usually feel compelled to care for their friends and neighbors more manifestly than other types due to their highly preferred use of extroverted feeling. The most famous ISFJ is good old Charlie Brown. Take note of how he manages his baseball team, takes care of his little sister, and how he interacts with his unusual dog.

Here's the math:

(-1x4)+(3x1)+(2x1)-(1x1)

-4+3+2-1

-5+5

O - Balanced

INTP - THE ARCHITECT

Introverted-Intuitive-Thinker-Perceiver

The logical leader of the pack, introverted intuition (Ti) is the primary cognitive function of this type. Ne, or extroverted intuition, is the secondary function, focusing on and exploring data and connections. Introverted sensing (Si) is in the tertiary position, providing mega memory for that great big nerdy brain. The inferior function is extroverted feeling (Fe), which is affected by the social atmosphere of the tribe.

Does this personality type seem a little nerdy to you? It should. These people actually love data. Once again we can turn to Charles Schultz to illustrate (literally) this character. Marcy is the quintessential INTP. If you prefer real life examples, Albert Einstein is the usual go-to person for this type.

Here's the data:

$(1x4)-(1x3)-(2x1)+(1x1)$

4-3-2+1

4-5+1

4-4

0 - Balanced

Chapter 8 - ENTP and ESFJ

Flying is learning how to throw yourself to the ground and miss.

- Douglas Adams

I knew what my job was. It was to go out, meet the people, and love them.

- Princess Diana

THE DEBATER and THE PROVIDER are the two extroverted types with balanced energies on the spectrum. One is focused on exploring new ideas, or old ideas in a new way. The other is more concerned with harmony of the tribe, family, friends, and coworkers.

ENTP - THE DEBATER

Extroverted-Intuitive-Thinker-Perceiver

Extroverted intuition (Ne) is the primary cognitive function, preoccupied with exploring connections, possibilities, and patterns in the outside world. The secondary function is Ti, or introverted thinking, providing internally focused logic for decision making. In the tertiary position is extroverted feeling (Fe), monitoring the atmosphere and camaraderie of the tribe. Si, or introverted sensing, is the inferior function, remembering the way things were and pining for the way things ought to be.

The ENTP is usually an outgoing, friendly person with the gift of gab. He doesn't ever mind playing the devil's advocate, even against his own ideas. TV's Dr. House, though not a friendly as most with this type, is a good example of The Debater.

Here's the math:

$(-1x4)+(3x1)+(2x1)-(1x1)$

-4+3+2-1

-5+5

0 - Balanced

ESFJ - THE PROVIDER
Extroverted-Sensor-Feeler-Judger

With a focus on the wellbeing and morale of the tribe, the primary cognitive function of The Provider is Fe, or extroverted feeling. The secondary function is the memory driven introverted sensing (Si), which focuses inwardly on detailed information by continually comparing it to the past or the way things should be. The tertiary function is extroverted intuition (Ne), noticing patterns and making connections. Rounding out the type is the inferior function, introverted thinking (Ti), analyzing situations with logic.

The ESFJ is very much a parent, always looking out for the good of the tribe. They thrive on being helpful, though are known to be just a tad gossipy. They have big mouths and big hearts. The late comic actor, Chris Farley, is a good example of this personality type. Also Patty (not Peppermint) from the Peanuts franchise, was probably based on an ESFJ person.

Here's the math:

(1x4)-(1x3)-(1x2)+(1x1)

4-3-2+1

1-1

0 - Balanced

Part Four Feminine Types

Chapter 9 - ENFP and ENFJ

I have affixed to me the dirt and dust of countless ages. Who am I to disturb history?

- Pig Pen

Take chances, make mistakes, get messy!

- Ms. Frizzle

The first two feminine types, nicknamed THE CHAMPION and THE MENTOR, both ranking a negative two on the spectrum. This would mean both masculine and feminine energies are quite present, but these personalities are located squarely in the feminine camp.

ENFP - THE CHAMPION

The Champion's primary cognitive function is extroverted intuition (Ne), which explores possibilities, patterns and connections. Fi, or introverted feeling is the secondary function, providing strong core personal values used to make decisions. Giving the ability to organize the outside world logically, extroverted thinking (Te) is the tertiary function. The less developed inferior function is introverted sensing (Si), which takes in details and simultaneously compares them to the past.

My favorite ENFP fictional character is Pig-Pen from the Peanuts franchise. He's a great champion of being yourself. If you happen to believe that he's not an ENFP, that's okay. You have the right to be wrong. I have seen some MBTI memes that classify him as an ISTP. That's not even close. Pig Pen is ENFP through and through.

Here's the down and dirty on the math:

(-1x4)-(1x3)+(3x2)-(1x1)

-4-3+6-1

-7+5

-2 - Feminine

ENFJ - THE MENTOR

Also known as THE TEACHER, THE MENTOR has extroverted feeling (Fe) in the primary position of the cognitive stack, focusing on the values and morale of the community and tribe and making decisions based on them. Introverted intuition (Ni) explores future possibilities and patterns, and is the secondary cognitive function. In the tertiary slot is Se, or extroverted sensing, an in-the-moment, detail oriented function. The inferior function Ti, or introverted thinking, is providing logical understanding to this lugubrious type.

Mrs. Frizzle from The Magic School Bus is a flamboyant example of this type. Charlie Brown's sister, Sally, is another quite animated ENFJ. They both have high expectations of others, and encourage others to be the best they can be, even if Sally does want to take Charlie Brown's room from him. I mean, just thing of all the possibilities!

Here's the math:

$(4x1)-(3x3)+(2x1)+(1x1)$

$4-9+2+1$

$-5+3$

-2 - Feminine

Chapter 10 - INTJ and ISFP

If you have what you say you have, I will make you rich. If you don't, I'll make you into shoes.

- Moriarty

Art is about building a new foundation, not just laying something on top of what's already there.

- Prince

The two types in the middle of the feminine side of the spectrum are THE MASTERMIND and THE ARTIST. Both are introverted, and both rank at negative four on the spectrum.

INTJ - THE MASTERMIND

Introverted intuition (Ni) is The Mastermind's primary cognitive function, planning well into the future and recognizing intricate, abstract patterns. The secondary function is extroverted thinking (Te), which organizes the outside world with logic and order, usually from the top down. Fortifying this personality type with strong inner values, introverted feeling (Fi) is the tertiary cognitive function. The less developed inferior function is extroverted sensing (Se), downloading concrete details from the outside world through the five senses.

Hollywood movies often use the INTJ stereotype to depict arch villains, like Dr. No or Moriarty. It's the quiet ones you have to watch out for, you know? Another more recent example of this personality type is Walter White from the TV series, Breaking Bad. This is why I've come to believe that the INTJ is one of the most misunderstood personality types.

Here's the math:

$(-3 \times 4)+(3 \times 3)-(2 \times 1)+(1 \times 1)$

$-12+9-2+1$

$-3-1$

-4 - Feminine

ISFP - THE ARTIST

The primary function is Fi, or introverted feeling, giving this type a strong core, just loaded with personal values and complex emotions. Extroverted sensing (Se) is the secondary function, placing ISFP's firmly in reality with a focus on the here-and-now. Introverted intuition (Ni), being the tertiary function, helps with recognizing complex patterns. The less developed inferior function is extroverted thinking (Te), helping them to organize their environment.

The Artist is very ... artistic. I personally know two ISFP's who are impressive at creating hand drawn signage, something I could never do even with years of training. They are usually nature lovers, more than most. They like find enjoy beauty in the world around them. The late musical genius, Prince, is believed to be an ISFP.

Here's the beautiful math:

$(-1x4)+(1x3)-(3x2)+(3x1)$

$-4+3-6+3$

$-10+6$

-4 - Feminine

Chapter 11 - INFP and INFJ

No problem is so big or so complicated that it can't be run away from.

- Linus Van Pelt

Each generation must be able to blame the previous generation for its problems. It doesn't solve anything, but it makes us all feel better.

- Lucy Van Pelt

THE HEALER and THE COUNSELOR are the two most feminine types, ranking a negative six on the spectrum. Notice the nurturing aspects of the two nicknames.

INFP - THE HEALER

The primary cognitive function is introverted feeling (Fi), providing this type with strong core values, incredibly complex emotions, and a rich inner world. The secondary function, extroverted intuition (Ne), perceives abstract connections from seemingly random places and things. Si, or introverted sensing is the tertiary function that relies heavily on memory and continually compares details in the current environment to the past. Extroverted thinking (Te) is the less developed inferior function, helping The Healer to organize the outside world, usually in the form of encouraging others.

The best example of an INFP is Linus Van Pelt from Charles Schultz Peanuts franchise. If you are an INFP or know one, you should study this character. You will be enlightened.

Here's the math:

$(-1x4)-(1x3)-(1x2)+(3x1)$

-4-3-2+3

-9+3

-6 - Feminine

INFJ - THE COUNSELOR

The primary cognitive function of The Counselor is introverted intuition (Ni), recognizing patterns and abstract ideas, then projecting their meaning and ramifications into the future. Extroverted feeling (Fe) is the secondary function, monitoring, making decisions by, and adjusting to the morale and values of the tribe. Introverted thinking (Ti) is in the tertiary slot, analyzing with reason and logic, both subjective and objective. The inferior function is Se, or extroverted sensing, which takes in detailed information with the five senses.

The Counselor is a person whom you feel perfectly comfortable sitting down in front of and then divulging your entire life story. Yes, this really happens to them all the time. A great example of this type is Lucy Van Pelt. Did you ever notice that she has a lot of customers in her nickel priced psychology practice? There's a good reason for that.

Here's the math:

(-3x4)+(3x1)+(2x1)+(1x1)

-12+6

-6 - Feminine

Part Five
The Breakdown

Chapter 12 - Discussion

Talk to me so you can see what's going on.

- Marvin Gaye

After doing the math, it's plain to see a spectrum from femininity to masculinity based on the cognitive functions. The spectrum goes from negative six to positive six. A perusal of the previous chapters would illuminate some interesting results.

Four of the six masculine types are sensor thinkers. The ESFP is the only masculine feeler and the ENTJ is the only type preferring intuition. Four of the six masculine types are extroverted. The ISTP and the ISTJ are the only two introverts on the masculine side of the spectrum (at positive two). Interestingly enough, the judgers and perceivers are equal in number interspersed through the entire spectrum.

There are four balanced types, two extroverts and two introverts. It was a little surprising to see that there are no sensor thinkers in this part of the spectrum. Both thinkers prefer intuition for their perceiving function. Both feelers prefer sensing. Like the masculine section of the spectrum, the number of perceivers and judgers are equal.

The vast majority of the NF temperament is feminine. There is only one sensor, the ISFP, and one thinker, the INTJ. Only two of the feminine types are extroverted, and they would be the least feminine on the spectrum (negative 2). Once again, the judgers and perceivers are equal in number.

For me, this spectrum left more questions than answers. I suppose that's a good thing. Since this thought experiment is based on quasi scientific models, it would be difficult to verify the accuracy of the spectrum. But there is one somewhat empirical test that can be applied, which is what the next section will cover. At this point I have no idea what the numbers will show. The next chapter will be written as I find out!

Chapter 13 - Population

The first step toward getting somewhere is deciding you're not going to stay where you are.

- JP Morgan

Assuming that most males are masculine and most females are feminine, the percentages of males and females of each personality type should reflect that. This is a broad, sweeping assumption for sure, but it's a good starting point.

There are several problems with this survey, though. First, the male and female percentages for each personality type vary widely depending on your chosen source. Also, there is always the possibility of people being mistyped. Of course, the scientific rigor, or lack thereof, concerning MBTI is a problem too.

With all this in mind, let's forge ahead anyway. We will look at a simplified model of the numbers taken from several sources. In other words, they will be averages of averages. But that's okay. This is simply a way to verify the plausibility of the spectrum. I don't think the world will be shaken with what was found.

Moving on - some research has now been done. I've taken some numbers from two websites (personalitycafe.com[1] and CAPT.org) and an old article. The article is taken from the Journal of Psychological Type back in 1996. Perhaps it's a little antiquated, but it comes pretty much directly from the MBTI horse's mouth, so to speak (Mitchell and Hammer). All three of these sources had similar findings with a few outliers here and there. I averaged the three percentages, which I rounded to whole numbers, to come up with a final number, stopping at the tenth percent. The final composite numbers are the estimated percentages of males and females of each personality type in the

---

1.   http://personalitycafe.com

US population. And now the moment of watered down truth, it's time to see how the spectrum stacks up. The next chapter will focus on the masculine types.

Chapter 14 - The Masculine Types

Every man's life ends the same way. It is only the details of how he lived and how he died that distinguish one man from another.

- Ernest Hemingway

The ESTP and the ESTJ both ranked at positive six on the spectrum. If most males are masculine, these two types should be overwhelmingly male population wise. According to the numbers, they are. The ESTJ takes up thirteen point three percent of the male and 8 percent of the female populations. This leaves a whopping five point three percent gap on the male side, which would make sense, because extroverted thinking is such a heavily masculine cognitive function.

What about the ESTP? While not as common a type as their judger cousins, The Negotiator takes up eight point three percent of the US male population and five percent of the female. This leaves a three point three percent surplus on the male side. While not as robust a discrepancy as before, the ESTP is holding the line, correlatively speaking. Not too shabby considering this type doesn't have extroverted thinking anywhere in its cognitive stack.

The ENTJ and ESFP both ranked a solid four on the masculinity scale. One would assume similar results, but perhaps not as robust. One would be wrong.

The ENTJ worked out perfectly well. About five percent of the population seems to be ENTJ males, and around two point six percent are ENTJ females. This leaves a difference of positive two point four, definitely a male result, so three for three.

But the ESFP went magnificently wrong. Approximately five point six percent of the population are ESFP males, and a whopping ten percent are females. This leaves quite a significant difference of negative four point four percent, which is totally female. Sometimes, back in the golden age of Hollywood or even Vaudville, a male entertainer was sometimes called a "dandy."

Perhaps these "dandies" were just flamboyant male ESFP's. At any rate, this type gets an asterisk for further review. It's just like an ESFP to want all that extra attention.

The two introverted masculine types, scoring a positive two on the spectrum, are the ISTJ and ISTP. They should have a slightly higher percentage of males to females in the population count. Someone should have told them what slight means.

The ISTJ is definitely male in nature. According to the numbers I obtained, seventeen point three percent of the population are ISTJ males and nine point three percent are females of this type. This leaves a huge positive eight percent gap leaning toward the males. While this type doesn't get the dreaded asterisk, I have to say that I'm dubious of the population numbers here. I don't for one second believe that almost one fifth of the population is an ISTJ male. This is the problem with typology. The theory is compelling, but the numbers can be quite sketchy. To be fair, quantifying people is kind of like herding cats in acid, so there's that.

The ISTP falls more in line with expectations. About eight point six percent of the US population are ISTP males. Only three point six percent are ISTP females. This is a difference of positive five percent, a male result, as one would expect.

So everything worked out on the masculine side of the spectrum, except for one type. More discussion is needed for the ESFP, but we will need to see how many more asterisks are accrued.

Chapter 15 - The Balanced Types

I have never in my life walked with a harness. The weight of the tether makes it feel like I'm dragging an anchor behind me.

- Nik Wallenda

There are four balanced types. Everything seems to balance out between them too. Half are extroverted, and the other half are introverted. Half are feelers, the other half are thinkers. There are two judging types and two perceiving types. Two of the types are intuitive, and the other two types are sensors. The question here, though, is - How this was reflected in the population? The ideal difference between the male and female percentages for these types would be zero. This, of course, did not happen, but they should be pretty darn close.

The ISFJ didn't even come close. The numbers I found had the male population at five point six percent and the female at fourteen point six percent. This left a huge nine percent difference, leaning way toward the female side. This is the first asterisk for the balanced types. Not the best start.

The INTP numbers faired much better. Five point six percent of the US population is male INTP, while two point three percent is female. This difference of three point three percent is much more in line with neutral expectations.

The ENTP statistics weren't too bad either. Six percent of the US population are ENTP males. Three percent are females. This is a three percent difference on the male side, which is close enough to zero for me.

Once again, we have a problem, those gossipy ESFJ's. Six point three percent are males, but fifteen percent are females.

This difference of negative eight point seven percent leans way toward the female camp and nowhere near zero. So the balanced types get two asterisks. It would appear that, all other things being equal, feelers naturally lean to female. What can I say here? Life is hard, and feelings are irrational.

Chapter 16 - The Feminine Types

Give a girl the right pair of shoes, and she'll conquer the world.

- Marilyn Monroe

There are six feminine types. Only two are extroverted. All the types with an NF temperament are represented. Only one sensor is found on this side of the spectrum. But will the population percentages agree?

The ENFJ and ENFP both ranked a negative two on the spectrum. These are the only extroverted feminine types. One would expect the population percentages to reflect a slightly higher female number. One would be correct.

The ENFP US male population percentage is six point three. The female number is eight point zero percent. The difference is negative one point seven percent, which is right on target, a slightly feminine number.

The ENFJ is similar to its perceiver cousin. The ENFJ male percentage is two point three. The female number is double that at four point six percent. The difference is negative two point three percent, a more significant, but still only slightly feminine leaning. Again, this is right on target.

The INTJ is the only thinker in the feminine side of the spectrum. Remember, all thinkers feel and all feelers think. Thinkers just prefer to utilize logic when making decisions before resorting to feelings or values. This particular thinker is hurting my brain, though. The male population percentages are four point zero. The female number is two point four percent. The difference is positive two point for percent, a woefully masculine leaning number. This personality type, one of the most misunderstood of the sixteen, gets an asterisk.

The ever so artistic ISFP also ranks a negative four on the spectrum, so THE ARTIST should get a solidly female percentage. This time the math works out pretty well. The male population number is four point three percent. The female number is seven point zero percent. This leaves a difference of negative two point seven percent, a solidly feminine result.

The two most feminine types, ranking a negative six on the spectrum, are the INFJ and INFP. Their numbers should, in both cases, lean toward a female result.

The INFJ's male population is one point six percent. The female number is two point six percent. This leaves a difference of negative one percent. This is definitely a feminine number, but not the overwhelming number one would expect. However, this is the rarest personality type, which could have a skewing effect. All in all, THE SAGE, also known as THE COUNSELOR, doesn't get the dreaded asterisk.

The INFP's male population is three point six percent. The female percentage is four point three. The difference is less than spectacular here at negative zero point seven. Again, this is a pretty rare personality type. The good news is that it's definitely a feminine number, so no asterisk needed, just a blanket and a teddy bear.

Chapter 18 - Patterns

This book has primarily focused on the personality characteristics through the lens of MBTI. It must be stated, however, that there are other personality typing systems. Socionics is basically the Russian (or former USSR) version of MBTI. The Big 5 is currently the golden child of personality psychology in some scientific circles. There is also the Enneagram, which is completely different, but is very much en Vogue right now. All of these have their merits and shortcomings. MBTI is my system of choice, because it describes patterns of thinking. It is, to my mind, the best personality typing system to incorporate the masculine and feminine energies. These energies are not metaphysical or even necessarily spiritual, though they have been described that way for centuries. They are patterns of behavior that are perceived by people due to patterns of thinking, also known as cognitive functions.

In a previous chapter, there was a short list of the Yin (feminine) and Yang (masculine) characteristics. It is not the purpose of this book to be the final arbiter of all the specific characteristics on the spectrum. We would all be in trouble if that were the case. I would be remiss, though, if I were to leave out a section describing some of them in more detail and how they mesh with the cognitive functions.

This masculine and feminine energies idea comes from Taoism. People believing in this philosophy see feminine and masculine energy in everything. Before I lose you here, understand that even many languages, Spanish for instance, apply gender to objects and even abstract ideas. So when we're talking about energies, it's merely a recognition of the innate characteristics of things. A common example used to explain this the description of a cup. It's material is hard, rigid, and unmoving, which is masculine in nature. But the emptiness and the capacity to hold and receive is feminine. A cup isn't a cup at all if it lacks either side of its energies. With this in mind, it becomes easy to extrapolate the idea of recognizing the masculine and feminine natures of more abstract ideas. These abstract characteristics of people are opposites of the same coin. They are complementary to one another, and both are necessary.

A quick look on the internet will afford you tons of Yin and Yang charts and symbols. From this search, one can begin to see patterns emerging. It must be stated, however, that some of these can be wrong. For instance, patience is actually a masculine energy, because it involves active self discipline. Many internet lists have erroneously placed it on the feminine side. (I know ladies, you've got to patient with us guys.) Be that as it may, a general list can easily be gleaned. A brief, and by no means complete, discussion is given below.

As far as perception goes, concrete thinking is masculine while intuition is feminine. Feminine leaning people would be nurturing (let me do that for you), while masculine people tend to be more supportive (you can do it). A masculine attitude would be more assertive (it needs to be this way), and a feminine attitude is more receptive (okay, if that's how it has to be). When accomplishing a task, feminine attitudes are usually collaborative (let's see what we can do), but masculine attitudes are more singularly focused (time for me to get this done). The masculine aspect of a personality would be more solid and stable. The feminine personality aspect would be more fluid and flexible. Masculine characteristics are steadfast (you can depend on me). Feminine characteristics are harmonious (we depend on each other). Masculine thinkers are logical and principled. Feminine thinkers are feeling and values oriented.

The discussion above only focuses on positive aspects of personality. There are dark, toxic energies too. Once again, I must state that I'm not a Taoist. I don't believe in ascension and enlightenment, at least not in the same way they do. It's all very well and good, but I believe in Jesus. I do, however, recognize the value and usefulness of the line of thought in this philosophy. I'm not about to falsely portray the life philosophy of millions of people. If this interests you, there are tons of books and videos on the subject. Have at it. Jesus is better than all of it, though. Just saying.

Now, back to the matter at hand. It's not hard to see how the cognitive functions can be ascribed masculine or feminine descriptions. Thinkers are logical, so they are masculine. Intuitive perception is feminine. Feeling and values are feminine. Extroverted thinking is forceful decision making organizing the outside world, so it's masculine. In short, Jungian psychological descriptions of the human psyche mesh almost perfectly with the Yin and Yang observations and thoughts of the Taoist philosophy. Jung himself spent a good deal of time investigating eastern philosophies to. He was particularly interested in mandalas, those circular spiritual illustrations that carried loads of symbolism and meaning, including masculine and feminine energies.

Chapter 19 - Wrap Up

Never give up, for that is just the place and time the tide will turn.

- Harriet Beecher Stowe

There were four types with asterisks. In other words, their male to female population numbers were not matching up to the expected numbers based on their places on the spectrum. The good news is that twelve of the sixteen types seemed to have the percentages and differences between the genders that one would expect, more or less. Seventy-five may be a C, but it's a passing score. Unfortunately, the four types in question, ESFP, INTJ, ISFJ, and ESFJ, have all scored nowhere near the target.

The ESFP is the only type on the masculine spectrum with a majority female population percentage. A difference of four point four percent would be a number that one would expect to see from a personality type scoring at least a negative two on the spectrum. Perhaps the introverted sensing, a feminine function in the second slot of the cognitive stack, is more influential than previously thought. Should it have a value of negative two instead of negative one? Quite honestly, it bothers me that none of the cognitive functions have a value of two, neither positive nor negative. There are reasons for this, but Dave and Shannon from Objective Personality (more about them to follow) have their reasons and methods too. In other words, I may be missing something here.

The only personality type on the feminine side with an asterisk is the INTJ. Speaking frankly, this one didn't really surprise me. THE MASTERMIND is one of the most misunderstood types. It's only fitting that it would continue to break the mold. It's just how they roll.

The XSFJ's, both THE PROVIDER and THE DEFENDER, who were supposed to be balanced, skewed way toward the female, population wise. This did surprise me. Sure, introverted sensing is a feminine cognitive function, but extroverted feeling is masculine. This makes me wonder if one cognitive function, higher in the cognitive stack, influences the masculinity or femininity of the less developed functions. While I don't agree with Chris from AsuraPsych, who only considers the first two functions, these two personality types definitely suggest that the spectrum needs some fine tuning. Maybe the multipliers in the formula should be tweaked, giving the first two functions an even greater value.

So what's to be learned from all this? It's hard to say, but I feel confident that the masculinity to femininity spectrum is plausible, at least as a basic model. There is no doubt, however, that it needs to be augmented in several ways. There needs to be more valid data too, but people are hard to quantify.

Chris from the YouTube channel, AusuraPsych, in addition to the website and YouTube channel, ObjectivePersonality (Dave and Shannon), are the two most accessible parties discussing masculinity and femininity in personality types. Between the two, I agree more with Chris. He believes the cognitive functions are inherently feminine or masculine. Dave and Shannon have a completely different theory based on their objective personality methods. I don't think they are wrong. Their data is their data. Chris' ideas just seem to be a better fit with the Jungian psychological model. Perhaps there will be a melding of the two theories over time as more and more trustworthy data become available. Maybe we'll all be blindsided by something completely different. Who knows?

I do disagree with Chris in this way. As stated before, he only considers the first two cognitive functions in the stack. I think all four should be considered, though not equally. (Many in the MBTI community would.) This is why I gave each function a multiplier of four down to one based on their place in the stack. I may be wrong here, but the lower functions are there and ought to be accounted for in some way. As stated before, the spectrum seems to be about seventy-five percent correct based on loose male to female population numbers. This is a good beginning, but really needs to be tightened up to meet more viable and useful standards. Perhaps the multipliers should have a greater divide, like seven for the primary, five for the secondary, three for the tertiary, and still one for the inferior function. While my multipliers seem arbitrary, they are more of a trial and error slash educated guess at this point. No doubt, real researchers and psychologists would have means to better data and methods.

It feels better to get this book written and out of my head. I truly want it to serve as a stepping stone for others who have better resources, and can further the discussion. If you're not sure about Jungian psychology or MBTI, there are tons of resources out there. I recommend PLEASE UNDERSTAND ME II by David Keirsey and PSYCHOLOGICAL TYPES by Carl Jung. The two YouTube channels discussed above are excellent resources, but there are many on the World Wide Web. I like LiJo, Frank James, Love Who, and Heart of Michi. These are fun, yet informative channels for those interested in personality psychology. Personality Junkie is a great website and podcast with plenty of information too. If you happened to enjoy this book (God help you), I wrote another called FROM THE PEANUTS SECTION that is a more basic description of the sixteen personality types. If you prefer to go straight to the horse's mouth, The Myers-Briggs Type Indicator is owned by a company called CCP Inc. To be clear, I'm not certified by that company, but I'm probably quite certifiable.

Masculine and feminine behavior patterns have been noticed by philosophers, especially in the Far East, for centuries. Much like the four elements and the four humors of ancient times, the observations were the best that could be done with what they had. While they didn't have access to microscopes or litmus tests, their work should not be ignored. To do so would be hubris. They had great wisdom based on deep thought. They recognized what made us who we are and described it to the best of their abilities. For that, we should be thankful .

I hope you enjoyed this book and learned something about personality. After all, we're all stuck in this great big world together. The more we can understand about each other, the better off we will all be. If you're already an MBTI nerd, I hope that I've done an adequate job of illustrating how the cognitive functions manifest with masculine or feminine energies. Maybe the combination of this knowledge with all that our new technologies have to offer will open up truer understanding. It could be that personality psychology will be able to stand up to scientific scrutiny and academic rigor in the near future. If you didn't enjoy this book, well, thanks for navel gazing with me.

Appendix
Sixteen MBTI TYPES ALONG THE SPECTRUM

-6	-4	-2	0	2	4	6
Most Feminine		Feminine	Neutral Balanced	Masculine		Most Masculine
INFP	INTJ	ENFP	ISFJ	ISTP	ESFP	ESTJ
THE	THE	THE	THE	THE	THE	THE
IDEALIST	MASTERMIND	CHAMPION	DEFENDER	CRAFTER	ENTERTAINER	MANAGER
INFJ	ISFP	ENFJ	INTP	ISTJ	ENTJ	ESTP
THE	THE	THE	THE	THE	THE	THE
COUNSELOR	ARTIST	TEACHER	ARCHITECT	INSPECTOR	EXECUTIVE	NEGOTIATOR
			ENTP			
			THE			
			DEBATOR			
			ESFJ			
			THE			
			PROVIDER			

There it is. This whole book compounded into one little chart, warts and all.

Remember that four of these personality types may need to be moved based on US population numbers. However, those numbers are likely ambiguous. Of the four questionable types, the INTJ and ESFP seem most out of place to my mind. Even so, they probably only need to be moved one or two spaces on the spectrum. Introverted feeling (Fi) would probably move THE ENTERTAINER down to positive two with the introverted masculine types. The INTJ's extroverted thinking (Te) may move this personality type from the feminine side to join the balanced personalities in the spectrum. Who knows, really? People are funny creatures.

Cover Photo Credit: Nila Coley

Don't miss out!

Visit the website below and you can sign up to receive emails whenever Jon Coley publishes a new book. There's no charge and no obligation.

https://books2read.com/r/B-A-OVTX-XXZJC

BOOKS 2 READ

Connecting independent readers to independent writers.

Also by Jon Coley

Schooling Abraham
Schooling Abraham
Tickled to Death: Funny Epitaphs for Kids
Numbskulls: Navigating Personality Conflicts
Anthology of Seasons
Skate or Die Jacob Jones
The Not So Great Divide

Watch for more at www.joncoleyauthor.com.

About the Author

Jon Coley lives in Georgia with his wife, daughters, an orange cat, an eccentric husky, and an overly affectionate a Great Dane. He has been a school teacher for more than two decades.

Read more at www.joncoleyauthor.com.